CHAMBERS HARRAP'S

PRIMARY SPANISH

TEACHERS' RESOURCE PACK

Published in Great Britain in 2006
by Chambers Harrap Publishers Ltd
7 Hopetoun Crescent
Edinburgh EH7 4AY

ISBN-13: 978 0550 10302 4
ISBN-10: 0550 10302 3

Authors
Daphne Day
Alison Sadler

Editor
Teresa Alvarez

Prepress
Heather Macpherson

Illustrations from Clipart.com

Designed and typeset by Chambers Harrap Publishers Ltd, Edinburgh
Printed and bound:
Hobbs the Printers Ltd, Totton, Hampshire

CHAMBERS HARRAP'S

This resource pack helps you and your class get the most out of ***Chambers Harrap's Primary Spanish Dictionary***: there's a page to accompany each scene, followed by 8 pages of photocopiable exercises (solutions on the inside front cover). You'll find information to brush up your own Spanish grammar, as well as lots of handy teaching tips and activity ideas to save you preparation time. Above all, this pack is designed to help you enjoy teaching Spanish, and your class to enjoy learning it!

¡HOLA NIÑOS!

Classroom Language

¡Hola niños!
Hello children!

¡Hola chicos/chicas!
Hello boys/girls!

¡Adiós niños!
Goodbye children!

¡Muy bien, niños!
Well done children!

¡Muy bien los verdes/los rojos!*
Well done the greens/the reds!

* *You can make names for teams using colour adjectives.*

Grammar Background

(*This is for your information – you may not want to make use of it in class*).

The Spanish word for *owl* is masculine – **el búho**, and this is why the owl says **Soy vuestro amigo**, using the masculine form of **amigo** (*friend*). If the bird was **una lechuza** (*a barn owl*), it would say **Soy vuestra amiga**.

Note that in Spanish you need an opening exclamation mark at the start of the phrase. The same applies for a question mark. (**¿Cómo estás?**)

Using the Dictionary

When a word is underlined in a speech bubble it means you'll find the whole sentence translated if you look up that word.

Get children to guess what a word means before looking it up – they will be keen to find out if they guessed right.

Get the class to look at the sentence **Voy a ayudaros a aprender español** (p.6) and ask them:

- Do we know any of these words?
- What do you think the sentence means? (*Write a couple of suggestions on the board*).

If the class are already competent dictionary users, ask them to look up **aprender**. If not show them the entry (p. 60).

➲ ***See pages 25 and 26 for photocopiable activities on alphabetical order.***

Language Awareness

Encourage children to spot the differences and similarities between Spanish and English: for example, in Spanish **animal** is spelt the same as *animal* in English but there are differences in pronunciation, and in Spanish the stress goes on the last syllable rather than the first.

Language Practice

Pick out children with names similar to Spanish ones, and get the class to pronounce them the Spanish way.

➲ ***See p. 7 for more information on Spanish names.***

Whole class practice

Teacher	**¡Hola Lucía!**
Lucía	**¡Hola!**
Whole class	**¡Hola Lucía!**
Lucía	**¡Hola!**

Group practice

Children take turns to say **¡Hola!**

Group replies, using the Spanish name or name pronounced in the Spanish way: **¡Hola Andrés!**, **¡Hola Rosa!** etc.

BUENOS DÍAS

Grammar Background

When you speak to one child you use a different form of the verb from when you speak to more than one:

¿cómo estás hoy, Juan? (literally *How are you today?* so the answer is **Bien, gracias**.)

¿cómo estáis hoy, niños?

When children speak to you they may use the more formal **usted** form (although in Spain they would often use the informal **tú** form):

¿cómo está hoy?

(!) *The verb **estar** (to be) is irregular: estoy, estás, está, estamos, estáis, estan.*

Classroom Language

¡Escucha, Marta!
Listen, Marta!

¡Escuchad (niños)!
Listen, children!

¡Mira la pizarra, Julia!
Look at the board, Julia!

¡Miradme (niños)!
Look at me, children!

¡Date prisa, Marcos!
Hurry up, Marcos!

¡Daos prisa (niños)!
Hurry up, children!

¡Vamos, Lucas!
Go on, Lucas!

¡Vamos (niños)!
Go on, children!

Language Practice

Check that the children say each other's names in a Spanish way.

Pair practice

Carolina **¿Cómo estás hoy, Samuel?**

Samuel **Bien, gracias, ¿y tú, Carolina?**

Carolina **Yo también.**

Whole class practice

The first child you point to asks the second child you point to:

¿Cómo estás hoy, Enrique?

Enrique replies and then asks the question to a third child:

Bien, gracias, ¿y tú, Carolina, cómo estás hoy?

The children can decide who they're going to ask, or you can point to someone.

Using the Dictionary

Look at the picture on p. 8 and see which words the class can guess the meaning of: **el champú**, **el sofá**, **una muñeca** will probably be no problem. **El tejado**, however, might be either *the tile*, or *the roof*, and **una habitación** may not be obvious at all, except that it's a something. When a problem word emerges, ask for suggested meanings and write them on the board. To speed up dictionary consultation, ask whereabouts in the dictionary the word will be – near the beginning, in the middle or towards the end? (If you haven't got the alphabet on the wall, you may want to write it on the board as a prompt.)

Muñeca will be in the middle of the dictionary, because it starts with **m**, which is in the middle of the alphabet.

Casa will be near the beginning, because **c** is near the beginning of the alphabet.

More Classroom Language

Buscad la palabra en el diccionario.
Look up the word in the dictionary.

en la página...
on page...

ES HORA DE VESTIRSE

➲ *See p. 26 for related photocopiable activities on alphabetical order.*

Grammar Background

Masculine and feminine

The most common form of ending for adjectives is **-o** (masculine) and **-a** (feminine):

un abrigo rojo
una falda amarilla

However, adjectives ending in **-e** such as **verde** and **triste**, or in a consonant such as **azul** or **gris** stay the same for both masculine and feminine, eg

una falda verde
un abrigo verde
una camiseta gris
un sombrero gris

Talking about items of clothing and personal possessions

In Spanish you use the article (**el**, **la**, **los** or **las**) when talking about items of clothing, rather than the equivalent of *my*:

Ponte los zapatos.
Put your shoes on.

Se puso la chaqueta.
He put his jacket on.

He perdido las llaves.
I've lost my keys.

Language Awareness

Un anorak is the same in English and Spanish. **Un pijama** is almost the same except that we don't say a pyjama in English!

Language Practice

1. ¿De qué color es... (*What colour is...*)

Ask the class about your clothes, adapting these questions to match what you're wearing:

¿De qué color es mi falda, blanca o negra?

¿De qué color es mi camiseta, verde o gris?

¿De qué color es mi jersey, amarillo o rosa?

¿De qué color es mi abrigo, rojo o verde?

¿De qué color son mis zapatos, negros o marrones?

ⓘ *El adjetivo **rosa** does not change ending for the masculine.*

2. Spanish children don't always wear school uniform. Get the class to describe theirs.

Write a heading on the board, and get the class to fill the gaps with colour words.

Nuestro uniforme (*Our uniform*)

un jersey ________

una camisa ________

unos pantalones ________

una falda ________

unos calcetines ________ **etc**

You could also talk about the uniform at another local school, and write the heading

El uniforme de...(*name of school*).

Alternatively make a poster showing a boy and girl in uniform, and label it.

EL DESAYUNO

Grammar Background

When you ask someone if they'd like some bread or some jam, you will see that *some* often has no equivalent word in Spanish, especially when it is followed by a singular noun:

¿Quieres pan?
Would you like some bread?

¿Quieres tostadas?
Would you like some toast?

Un poco de can sometimes be used:

¿Quieres (un poco de) café?
Would you like some coffee?

¿Puedo coger (un poco) de pan?
Can I have some bread?

ⓘ *Note that **cereales** and **tostadas** are plural in Spanish. **Una tostada** = a piece of toast*

Using the Dictionary

Ask the class:

¿Quieres una rana?

If nobody knows what the word means, ask the class to look it up to see if it's something they'd like to eat. If anyone does know the word, the answer will probably be **¡NO GRACIAS**!

¿Quieres un ratoncito?

Again, get the children to use the dictionary. At the entry, they'll find the phrase **un ratoncito, ñam, ñam…** This is the opinion of the owl.

➲ ***See p. 27 for photocopiable activities on "Sí, por favor" and "No gracias".***

Classroom Language

Siéntate, Pedro, por favor.
Sit down please, Pedro.

Sentaos niños, por favor.
Sit down please, children.

Una vez más, por favor, Ana.
(Do it) one more time please, Ana.

Una vez más, por favor, niños.
One more time please, children.

Language Practice

Write the following headings and lists on the board.

para beber	para comer
leche	cereales
zumo	tostadas
té	pan
leche caliente	miel
leche fría	mermelada

Practise questions and answers, pointing to the different options to get the **Sí** or **No** responses:

¿Quieres leche?

Sí, por favor.
No, zumo, por favor.
No, té, por favor.

¿Quieres cereales?

Sí, por favor.
No, tostadas, por favor.
No, pan, por favor.

¿Quieres leche o mermelada?
Mermelada, por favor.

¿Quieres leche caliente o leche fría?
Leche fría, por favor.

Language Awareness

In Spain people actually tend to use **por favor** very sparingly!

VAMOS A LA ESCUELA

Grammar Background

The expression **es hora de...** (*it's time to...*) is used with the infinitive (the form of the verb that appears in the dictionary). Some verbs (called reflexive verbs) have **se** as part of their infinitive, eg **levantarse** (*to get up*), **sentarse** (*to sit down*), **vestirse** (*to get dressed*). This **se** goes before the verb when not in the infinitive.

Es hora de levantarse.
It's time to get up.

Es hora de vestirse.
It's time to get dressed.

Es hora de ir a la escuela.
It's time to go to school.

Es hora de dejar de trabajar.
It's time to stop work.

➲ ***Listen to the song "Tic Toc" on the CD-ROM for more practice with "Es hora de...".***

Language Practice

1. Practise these questions and answers with the children (remember to pronounce their names the Spanish way):

Teacher	**¿Vienes David?**
David	**Ya voy(, señorita)**
Teacher	**¿Vienes Sara?**
Sara	**Ya voy(, señorita).**

2. Draw a clock showing 8 o'clock and label it **Es hora de ir a la escuela**. Practise saying the sentence.

Draw another clock showing the time the Spanish lesson starts, and label it **Es hora de aprender español**.

- Do the children remember this from the **¡Hola niños!** section?
- If not, ask what it could mean – what verb could go with **español**?

Language Awareness

1. If your class are familiar with grammatical terms, ask them which of the words they've been practising are verbs (**vienes**, **voy**, **ir**, **aprender**). If they suggest words which AREN'T verbs, revise nouns, adjectives and verbs.

- A noun is a thing, person, or place eg bag, mum, Spain.
- An adjective tells you about a thing, person or place eg yellow, ready, interesting.
- A verb is a doing word, eg come, go, learn, wait.

The Spanish words they know for clothes, animals and things to eat are nouns.

Can they think of some?

The Spanish words they know for colours are adjectives.

How many can they remember?

2. Simon says: Put your hand up if you hear a verb!

Teachers are always telling children to do things, so they use a lot of verbs:

¡Escuchad, niños! (*Listen, children*!);

¡Mirad, niños! (*Look, children*!);

¡Date prisa, Marcos! (*Hurry up, Marcos!*)

Read out the following sentences and tell the class to put their hands up if they hear a verb.

¡Sentaos, niños!

Adiós, mamá.

¡Muy bien, Lucía!

¡Muchas gracias!

Ya voy papá.

¡Escúchame Jaime!

¡Espérame!

¡Perdona!

EN CLASE

Grammar Background

The date is written like this in Spanish: **viernes, 3 de mayo** (*Friday 3 May*).

To say what the date is, you say:

Estamos a tres de mayo (*it's the third of May*).

You don't need to use **el**. The names of days of the week and months are NOT written with capitals in Spanish.

To say all the days of the month you just use the numbers **uno, dos, tres, cuatro** etc, so children need to know the numbers up to 31 to talk about dates:

Estamos a uno de mayo (*it's the first of May*).

Estamos a treinta de noviembre (*it's the thirtieth of November*).

Language Awareness

Look at the poster on the wall of the classroom (p. 16). Which of the words are nearly the same as English? (**un rectángulo**, **un triángulo**, **un círculo**, **el centro**). Is the meaning the same as in English?

Las figuras looks like English too – but why aren't there any figures on the poster? It's because **una figura** in Spanish means a shape, and not a number.

Looking at the rest of the picture, can you find four words which are nearly the same as English? (**clase, diccionario, calculadora, papel**)

If anyone suggests **profesor** (*teacher*) you can agree that the word is like professor, but **un profesor** teaches at a school, not a university.

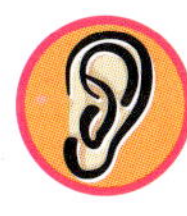

Pronunciation

To reinforce the point that words that look similar in Spanish are pronounced differently, make sure that in the Spanish lesson names are pronounced in a Spanish way. Check that the stress goes on the second syllable of the following names: David, Samuel, Daniel.

Children whose names haven't got a Spanish equivalent might like to choose a Spanish one.

Girls' names: Lucía, María, Paula, Laura, Marta, Sara, Andrea, Ana, Claudia, Irene, Cristina, Natalia, Elena, Alicia.

Boys' names: Alejandro, Daniel, Álvaro, Pablo, Adrián, Javier, Sergio, Jorge, Carlos, Diego, Mario, Miguel, Jaime, Iván.

Language Practice

Pronounce children's names in an English way and let them correct your pronunciation.

Practise **¡Que no!** first, making it very emphatic.

Teacher	**¿Te llamas David?**
David	**¡Que no! Me llamo David.**
Teacher	**¿Te llamas Paula?**
Paula	**¡Que no! Me llamo Paula.**
Teacher	**¿Te llamas Samuel?**
Samuel	**¡Que no! Me llamo Samuel.**
Teacher	**¿Te llamas Rose?**
Rosa	**¡Que no! Me llamo Rosa.**

¡VAMOS A ESTUDIAR MATEMÁTICAS!

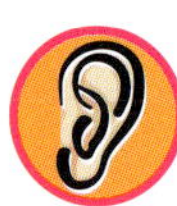

Pronunciation

In numbers like *a hundred and one*, *six hundred and eighty-four* or *two thousand and eighty* the word *and* is inserted in English. This does not happen in Spanish, eg **dos mil cuatro**, **ciento uno**.

Grammar Background

Saying how old you are

In Spanish you use the verb **tener** (*to have*) with ages.

¿Cuántos años tienes?
How old are you?

Tengo diez años.
I'm ten (years old).

Tomás tiene once años.
Tomás is eleven (years old).

Note that in Spanish, the number must be followed by the word **años** (*years*).

Classroom Language

¡Vamos a hacer un concurso!
Let's have a quiz!

un equipo
a team

¡Bien! ¡Es la respuesta correcta!
Good! That's the right answer!

¡Lo siento! ¡Esa respuesta está mal!
Sorry! That's the wrong answer!

un punto
a point

Has ganado dos puntos, Lucía.
You've scored two points, Lucía.

Los rojos tienen veinte puntos.
The reds have twenty points.

Los verdes tienen veintiséis puntos.
The greens have twenty-six points.

¡Han ganado los verdes!
The greens have won!

Language Practice

You can use quizzes to revise any aspect of language. You might want to give extra points for pronunciation – this will help to motivate the children. Keep the score in Spanish.

If children accuse each other of cheating, make them do it in Spanish:

¡(Estás haciendo) trampa!
You're cheating!

¡No hagas trampa!
Don't cheat!

You could ask questions in English (*What's the Spanish for...?*) or in Spanish – here are some suggestions:

Un bolígrafo, ¿qué es?
(*what is it?*)
(a pen)

¿Es una mesa o una puerta?
(*point to one of two alternatives*)
(eg "**una puerta**")

Esta chaqueta, ¿de qué color es?
(*what colour is it?*)
(eg "**negra**")

¿Cuántos son?
(*point to numbers written on board*)
(eg 17: "**diecisiete**")

¿A qué día estamos hoy?
(*point to dates written on board*)
("**estamos a...**")

You can also practise listening comprehension, giving children points for carrying out the instruction correctly:

¡Andrés, mira el ordenador!

¡Sonia, mira mis zapatos!

¡SONRÍE!

Grammar Background

Giving orders

The verbs Miguel uses as he takes the photos are in the **tu** form: **¡salta!**; **¡siéntate!**; **¡cierra los ojos!**.

If you want to address someone more formally, when children speak to their teacher for example, you use the **usted** form, which changes the final vowel in the imperative: **¡salte!**; **¡siéntese!**; **¡cierre los ojos!**

(Remember that in Spain children are likely to use the **tú** form of the verb with their teacher.)

If you want to tell the whole class to do something, you use the **vosotros** form: **¡saltad!**; **¡sentaos!**; **¡cerrad los ojos!**; **¡coged los libros!**.

Some Spanish imperatives end with **-te**, **-se** or **-os**: **date/dese/daos la vuelta**; **siéntate/siéntese/sentaos** (literally saying *turn yourself around*; *sit yourself down*). These imperatives are derived from reflexive verbs. Any verb shown in the dictionary with **se** at the end, such as **llamarse** (*to be called*) or **sentarse** (*to sit down*), is reflexive and has **-te**, **-se** or **-os** on the end of the imperative.

Parts of the body

As we will see in the section "***En el hospital***", when you talk about parts of the body in Spanish you generally use **el, la**, **los** or **las** rather than the equivalent of *my* or *your*: **¡Levanta el pie izquierdo!** (*lift your left foot!*); **¡Levanta la mano, por favor!** (*put up your hand, please!*); **¡Abrid los ojos!** (*open your eyes!*).

Classroom Language

¡Levanta la mano, Ana!
Put up your hand, Ana.

¡Levantad la mano!
Put up your hands, children.

(!) *Note that you use the singular* ***la mano*** *even when talking to more than one person.*

¡Inténtalo, Laura!
Try, Laura!

¡Intentadlo!
Try, children!

Language Awareness

There are lots of verbs in this scene, and not many nouns.

Do a sorting exercise with the whole class, writing lists like these on the board.

verbs	nouns
salta	**el pie**
levanta	**la nariz**
coge	**el libro**
tócate	**los ojos** etc.

Children can do the actions as they do the sorting exercise.

To help with dictionary skills, get the children to put the above lists into alphabetical order. This can be done as a class activity or in pairs or groups – see how many they can do in 5 minutes.

Language Practice

Pair practice

Children tell each other to do things, using the **tu** form: **¡Cierra los ojos!**; **¡Llora!** etc.

Whole class practice

Teacher tells the whole class to do things: **llorad**; **cerrad los ojos**; **abrid los ojos**; **reíd**; **tocaos la nariz**; **saltad**; **daos la vuelta**; **levantaos**.

Then pick children to tell you to do things – **Siéntese** (o **Siéntate**); **Cierre** (or **Cierra**) **los ojos** – but only do what they ask if they use the correct form of the verb.

EL CHICO NUEVO

Grammar Background

Masculine and feminine

Nuevo is an adjective meaning *new*. The feminine of **nuevo** is **nueva** – so *a new girl* is **una chica nueva**. Other adjectives that appear in this scene are **baja**, **gorda**, **delgada** and **alto**.

The two adjectives that are used for *older* and *younger* are **mayor** and **menor**. The masculine and feminine forms have the same ending and -**es** is added to form the plural:

Mi hermano mayor.
My older brother./My big brother.

Mi hermano es mayor que yo.
My brother is older than me.

Mi hermana menor.
My younger sister.

However the adjective **pequeño** is normally used instead of **menor** in everyday language:

Mi hermana pequeña.
My little sister.

Tengo tres hermanos más pequeños.
I have three younger brothers.

Language Practice

Do a survey of the whole class, getting children to shout out **¡yo!** when they fit into a particular category. Write all the categories (**un hermano pequeño** etc) on the board and count up the totals in Spanish.

¿Quién tiene un hermano pequeño?
(Who's got a little brother?)

¿Quién tiene un hermano mayor?
(Who's got a big brother?)

¿Quién tiene una hermana pequeña?
(Who's got a little sister?)

¿Quién tiene una hermana mayor?
(Who's got a big sister?)

When you've finished the survey you'll have your headings and totals on the board. Ask the children to compare **un hermano pequeño** and **una hermana pequeña,** and **un hermano mayor** and **una hermana mayor.**

- What is the difference in spelling?
- Did they notice the adjective that is the same in the masculine and the feminine?

Using the Dictionary

Words that change in the feminine

To find out whether an adjective is different in the feminine you can look it up in the dictionary. For example, look up **alto** – what do you find?

The feminine form is **alta**.

Now look up **feliz**. You will see this doesn't change in the feminine.

If you look up some of the other adjectives in this scene (**baja, delgada, gorda**) you might not see them immediately because in a Spanish dictionary the masculine form appears first, although in this dictionary the feminine form is given in full, which makes it easier to spot.

The children should now be able to complete these sentences:

Mario is fat.	**Mario es _ _ _ _ _.**
Ana is fat.	**Ana es_ _ _ _ _.**
Mario is happy.	**Mario es _ _ _ _ _.**
Ana is happy.	**Ana es _ _ _ _ _.**
Mario is short.	**Mario es _ _ _ _.**
Ana is short.	**Ana es _ _ _ _.**

LAS PROFESIONES

Grammar Background

In Spanish you don't translate *a* when you say *He's a taxi driver*, or *She's a doctor* **(Él) es taxista; (Ella) es médico.**

With some jobs the same word is used for men and women; with others there are different masculine and feminine forms:

un camarero a waiter
→ **Mi hermano es camarero.**
My brother is a waiter.

una camarera a waitress
→ **Mi hermana es camarera.**
My sister is a waitress.

un enfermero a (male) nurse
→ **Carlos es enfermero.**
Carlos is a nurse.

una enfermera a (female) nurse
→ **(Ella) es enfermera.**
She's a nurse.

Other examples are **informático/ informática** (*programmer*), **peluquero/ peluquera** (*hairdresser*), **abogado/ abogada** (*lawyer*), **profesor/profesora** (*teacher*).

➲ ***See p. 28 for a photocopiable exercise about "Las profesiones".***

Classroom Language

¿Quién lo sabe?	Who knows?
¿Nadie?	Nobody?
Yo lo sé.	I know.
No, no lo sé.	No, I don't know.

Language Awareness

Lots of Spanish words are almost the same as English ones. Can the children think of any?

There may be some on the walls of the classroom.

The 20 word challenge!

Tell the children you're going to read a list of 20 Spanish words (see opposite) to see how many of the meanings they can guess. Tell them to put their hands up when they hear a word they don't understand. Write these words on the board under the heading: Words we couldn't guess. The aim is to have as few words on this list as possible.

artista, actor, doctor, peluquero, guitarrista, carnicero, dentista, arquitecto, fotógrafo, fontanero, informático, mecánico, pianista, piloto, pintor, cocinero, taxista, electricista, deportista, jardinero.

The underlined words are those they probably won't recognise. They should know the rest.

Clues

Use these clues to help the children make sense of the unfamiliar words, and encourage them to have as few words as possible under the heading Words we couldn't guess.

- **Pelo** in Spanish means *hair*. So what job does a **peluquero** do? (*hairdresser*)
- In English a *carnivore* is an animal that eats *meat*. The children may even have heard of a dish we call by its Spanish name **chile con carne**. If the job a **carnicero** does involves handling *meat*, what job do you think it is? It's a type of shopkeeper. (*butcher*)
- **Informático** is very like the English word *information*. What sort of people work with *information* or *data*? The children may suggest *librarian* but in this case it's a computer expert. (*programmer*).
- **Cocinero** is related to another Spanish word: **cocina** (*kitchen*). What is someone called whose job is based in a kitchen? (*chef*)
- If you knock off the **de** from **deportista** and start the word with an **s** instead, you can see the similarity with an English word. **Deporte** in Spanish means *sport*. (*sportsperson*)
- Change the **j** of **jardinero** into a **g**, the **i** into an **e** and knock off the final **o** and what do you get? (*gardener*)

¿QUÉ HORA ES?

Language Practice

Listen to the song ***Tic, toc*** on the CD and get the children to sing it – as many times as they like, so that they master **las seis de la mañana, las ocho de la mañana, las doce del mediodía, las cuatro de la tarde** and **las diez de la noche**.

Pair activity

Write these times on the board: 6a.m., 8a.m., 12a.m., 4p.m., 10p.m.

Pairs practise saying the Spanish for them to each other.

Whole class activity 1

Spanish people sometimes use the 24-hour clock when telling the time, instead of saying a.m. and p.m.. Do the children know how it works?

To work out p.m. times by the 24-hour clock, you have to add 12 – so **las cuatro de la tarde** (4 p.m.) is **cuatro más doce** = **dieciséis horas**, which is written 16h.

Put some times on the board and get the class to work out their 24-hour clock:

1 p.m.	**la una**	=	**las trece horas 13h**
2 p.m.	**las dos**	=	**las catorce horas 14h**
3 p.m.	**las tres**	=	**las quince 15h**
10 p.m.	**las diez**	=	**las veintidós horas 22h**

Whole class activity 2

Write some key times from the school day on the board, and get children to say them. Then fill in what happens at each time. The song has given them the language for going to school, having dinner and going home. You may want to add breaktime (**el recreo**).

Un día normal *(An average day)*

9h Es hora de .... **(ir a la escuela)**

10h Es hora del .... **(recreo)**

12h Es hora de .... **(comer)**

15h Es hora de.. **(ir a casa)**

Bingo

Bingo is a good way of practising numbers and times. Use ready-made cards if you have them. If not, you can practise times as follows.

Divide the class into two teams (or more if you have a big class) such as **los búhos y las águilas** (the owls and the eagles), and give each team six times to write down:

los búhos

2 p.m. 4 a.m. 5 p.m. 6 a.m. 9 p.m. 11 a.m.

las águilas

11 p.m. 3 p.m. 5 p.m. 7 a.m. 9 a.m. 6 a.m.

You say the following times, twice each, and the teams cross out their numbers when they hear them. Tell them to shout **bingo!** when all their numbers are crossed out:

Las cinco de la tarde, las diez de la noche, las dos de la tarde, las seis de la mañana, las doce de la mañana, las tres de la mañana, las nueve de la mañana, las cuatro de la tarde, las siete de la mañana, las nueve de la tarde, las once de la mañana, las tres de la tarde, las ocho de la tarde, la una, las once de la noche.

Bingo ¡Han ganado las águilas!

You can play a similar game with dates, or use more complicated times, such as **las ocho y media, las seis y cuarto, las seis menos cuarto** etc.

EL GRAN PARTIDO

Grammar Background

When you talk about a sport in Spanish you use the definite article (*the* – **el**/**la**):

Me gusta el tenis.
I like tennis.

El fútbol es mi deporte preferido.
Football is my favourite sport.

When you talk about playing a sport or game you use the verb **jugar** followed by **al**:

Javier juega al squash.
Javier plays squash.

Elena juega al fútbol.
Elena plays football.

The **al** becomes **a los/las** if the word for the game is plural:

¿Quieres jugar a las cartas?
Do you want to play cards?

Juego a los dardos.
I play darts.

When you talk about playing a musical instrument you use the verb **tocar** followed by **el** if the instrument is a masculine word or **la** if the instrument is a feminine word:

Pablo toca el piano.
Pablo plays the piano.

Nuria toca la guitarra.
Nuria plays the guitar.

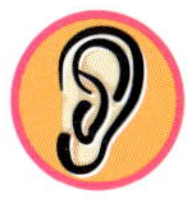

Pronunciation

Squash is an English word that has been assimilated into the Spanish language. Although it is spelt the same, the Spanish have their own two-syllable pronunciation for it: *"eskwas"*. The stress goes on the second syllable and **–was** rhymes with the animal *ass*. In **el tenis** and **el ping-pong**, the **i** rhymes with the **e** in *sheet*. When you say **hockey** in Spanish, the **–ey** rhymes with the English word *say*.

➲ ***See p. 29 for a photocopiable exercise about rhymes.***

Language Practice

The illustrations for ***"El gran partido"*** show that lots of English words (or adaptations of them) are used in the world of sport. The class can guess what rugby, hockey and golf are in Spanish – yes, **el rugby**, **el hockey** and **el golf**! **El ciclismo** (*cycling*) is a very popular Spanish sport – this word has not been borrowed from English!

Un sondeo (*A survey*)

Write the names of the sports you have talked about on the board, like this:

el fútbol	el golf
el ping-pong	el squash
el tenis	el rugby

Ask a few individuals:

Teacher **¿Alejandro, juegas al fútbol?**

Alejandro **Sí, sí juego.**

Teacher **¿Ana, juegas al fútbol?**

Ana **No, no juego.**

Then you can ask the whole class: **¿Quién juega al fútbol?**.

Get someone to count in Spanish, and write the total under **el fútbol**.

Do the same with the other sports. The answer to **¿quién juega al golf?** might be **nadie** (nobody), and the total **cero**.

Finally, declare the result of the survey: **El juego que más se practica es** ________.

You could do a similar survey on the musical instruments children play. Then the questions would use **tocar** (**¿Quién toca el violín?**, **¿Tocas la trompeta?**)

EN EL HOSPITAL

Grammar Background

Talking about things that hurt

In Spanish you generally use the definite article (**el**, **la**, **los** or **las**) when talking about parts of the body, rather than the equivalent of *my*: **la pierna**, not **mi pierna**.

Me duele la pierna.
My leg hurts.

Me duele el pie.
My foot hurts.

Me duelen los brazos.
My arms hurt.

Me duele la muela.
I've got toothache.

Me duele la cabeza.
I've got a headache *or* My head hurts.

Me duele el estómago.
I've got stomachache.

Note that in these phrases, as with **gustar**, you use the personal pronoun followed by the verb in the third person singular (*me duele, te duele, le duele, nos duele, os duele, les duele*) or plural, if the part of the body is plural (*me duelen, te duelen, le duelen, nos duelen, os duelen, les duelen*). When asking someone what's wrong with them, you use the reflexive form of **pasar**:

¿Qué te pasa, David?
What's wrong with you, David?

¿Qué os pasa, niños?
What's wrong with you, children?

¿Qué te pasa en la mano?
What's wrong with your hand?

¿Qué le pasa en la pierna a Tomás?
What's wrong with Tomás's leg?

Language Practice

Whole class practice

Ask the children what noise they make when something hurts. In Spanish you say **¡ay!** (*"ay!"*). See which half of the class can say it with most expression.

Then clutch your head and groan: **¡Ay, me duele la cabeza!**

Get the whole class to repeat it after you a couple of times, and then have half the class say it, then the other, competing to express most pain.

Do the same with other body parts: **¡Ay, me duele el dedo/la espalda** etc.

Pair practice

Explain to the class that **¿Qué te pasa?** is how you ask what's wrong. Practise it and then have this dialogue with one or two children:

Teacher **¿Qué te pasa, Emma?** (Gesturing to head/stomach/teeth etc)

Emma **Me duele la cabeza.**

Teacher **¡Pobre Emma!**

Children can then practise in pairs, taking turns to ask and answer and using all the phrases from the whole class practice.

Game

In the ***Las partes del cuerpo*** song on the CD there are phrases you can use to play a version of Simon Says: **¡Levanta las manos!** (*Put up your hands!*); **¡Saca la lengua!** (*Stick out your tongue!*); **¡Estira los brazos!** (*Stretch your arms!*); **¡Mueve la pierna!** (*Move your leg!*) etc. (If this is too many verbs for the class, use **Toca** with all the parts of the body. In this case you would normally say **Tócate la nariz**, although in the song you will hear **Toca tu nariz**.)

Divide the class into teams. Explain that you're going to tell people to do things, but they should only do them if you are polite and say **por favor**. If you don't, they say **¡No!**.

Teacher **Mueve la cabeza, Juan**

Juan **¡No!** (*1 point for his team*)

Teacher **Mueve la cabeza, por favor, Juan**

Juan *moves his head* (*1 point for his team*)

Teacher **Saca la lengua, por favor, Nuria.**

Nuria **No!** (*0 points for her team*)

EL ESCONDITE

Grammar Background

Unlike nouns, adjectives and verbs, words like **dentro de** (*inside*), **sobre** (*on*), **debajo de** (*under*), **delante de** (*in front of*), **enfrente de** (*opposite*), **cerca de** (*near*), always stay the same, but watch out for the combinations **de** + **el** → **del** and **a** + **el** → **al**:

Está cerca del castillo.
It's near the castle.

Vamos al servicio.
We're going to the toilet.

When you want to say that something is in a room, cupboard, bag etc you use the preposition **en** in Spanish: on p. 32 you can see that **El gato está en la caja** (*The cat is in the box*). Notice that the cat sitting in the box on top of that one is also *in the box* but he is described as being **dentro de la caja**. This just means he is *inside* it as opposed to *outside* it. If you look up **en** in the dictionary you will see that it can also mean *on*: **el gato está durmiendo en el sofá** (*the cat is sleeping on the sofa*).

Language Practice

Talk about where people sit in class using these prepositions: **entre** (*between*), **delante de** (*in front of*), **detrás de** (*behind*), **enfrente de** (*opposite*), **al lado de** (*next to*).

Simón está entre Marcos y Cristóbal.

Marta está delante de Juan Carlos.

Julia está al lado de Eloísa.

¿Verdadero o falso? *(True or false?)*

Teacher **¿Marcos está entre Simón y Cristóbal?**

Class **¡No, falso!**

Teacher **¿Cristóbal está al lado de Simón?**

Class **¡Sí, verdadero!**

You can do the same sort of thing with a picture – first discuss where the people or things are, and then make statements about them that are true or false.

¿Quién es? (*Who is it?*)

(*NB: Don't look at the person you're describing!*)

Teacher **Está delante de mí – ¿quién es?**

Class **¡Es Andrés!**

Teacher **Está entre Miguel y Julia – ¿quién es?**

Class **¡Es Carmen!**

Children can also do this activity in pairs.

¿Dónde estás? (*Where are you?*)

Teacher **¿Dónde estás, Cecilia?**

Cecilia **Estoy enfrente de Pedro.**

Teacher **¿Dónde estás, Diego?**

Diego **Estoy detrás de María.**

¿Dónde está el oso? (*Where is the bear?*)

Use a soft toy and a bag or box to demonstrate a variety of prepositions: **el oso** (*or other toy*) **está encima de la mesa/en mi cabeza/debajo de la silla/en mi jersey/dentro de la caja/detrás de Sam/delante de la pizarra**. You can move the toy around, asking **¿Y ahora, dónde está el oso?**.

Guessing game

Hide a familiar object in the classroom before the lesson. Tell the children this object (eg **el oso**) is hidden, and get them to guess where it is: **¿Está dentro del bolso?, ¿Está en el cajón?, ¿Está detrás de la puerta?, ¿Está en el armario?, ¿Está debajo de la mesa?**.

EN LA CIUDAD

Grammar Background

Speaking politely

Elena politely says **Perdone.** She could have said **Perdona**, since it is normal in Spanish to address a stranger using the informal **tú** form. Her response to the **policía** should be **Gracias**. For *You're welcome!* you can say **¡De nada!**.

The policeman replies to Elena using the informal **tú** form of **seguir** (**sigue**) and **coger** (**coge**) because she is younger.

Asking the way

A phrase you often hear when someone tells you the way is **todo recto** (*straight on*). The adjective **derecho** means both *straight* and *right*: **el brazo derecho** (*the right arm*), **la mano derecha** (*the right hand*). The nouns **la derecha** and **la izquierda** are also used when giving directions: **a la derecha** (*on the right* or *to the right*) and **a la izquierda** (*on the left* or *to the left*).

ⓘ *Note that* **derecha** *is the feminine form of the adjective as well as a feminine noun.*

Language Practice

Whole class activity: left and right/ putting words into action

For this activity, it doesn't matter if they don't know all the verbs – you can teach them as you go along. They'll know **poned** by the end of the activity!

¡Levantad la mano izquierda!
Put up your left hand!

¡Levantad la mano derecha!
Put up your right hand!

¡Poned la mano izquierda encima de la cabeza!
Put your left hand on your head!

¡Poned la mano derecha en la barriga!
Put your right hand on your tummy!

¡Poned la mano izquierda encima del brazo derecho!
Put your left hand on your right arm!

¡Poned las manos sobre la mesa!
Put your hands on the table!

¡Poned las manos en los ojos!
Put your hands over your eyes!

¡Poned la mano derecha en la boca!
Put your right hand over your mouth!

¡Poned la mano derecha en el ojo derecho!
Put your right hand over your right eye!

¡Poned la mano izquierda en el ojo derecho!
Put your left hand over your right eye!

¡Cerrad el ojo derecho!
Shut your right eye!

¡Cerrad el ojo izquierdo!
Shut your left eye!

¡Mirad a la izquierda!
Look to the left!

¡Mirad a la derecha!
Look to the right!

Language Awareness

"Coge la tercera calle a la derecha y después la segunda calle a la izquierda."

- Which streets does the policeman tell Elena to take? If children don't recognise the words **segunda** and **tercera**, ask them if they look like any English words. **Segunda** is very similar to *second* and **tercera** has **t**, **r** and **e** in it, the same as the English *three*, but as we are talking about ordinal numbers rather than the cardinal numbers we looked at in **Vamos a estudiar matemáticas**, it would be *third*.
- If you look at p. 96 you will see that the Spanish ordinal numbers are shown with a masculine **–o** ending. When they are used as adjectives they can be either masc-uline or feminine, depending on the noun following them: **la tercera calle**, **el segundo semáforo** etc.
- What do you put on the end of English numbers, which is like **–o** and **-a** in Spanish? (**-th**, eg fourth).

EN EL SUPERMERCADO

Grammar Background

When you talk about your general likes and dislikes in Spanish you always use the definite article, **el**, **la**, **los** or **las** – that's why Miguel says "**Me encanta <u>el</u> helado**".

¿Te gustan las fresas?
Do you like strawberries?

Sí, me gustan todas las frutas.
Yes, I like all fruit.

Me encantan las peras.
I love pears.

No me gusta el queso.
I don't like cheese.

No me gustan los tomates.
I don't like tomatoes.

(!) *Note that in Spanish, **una fruta** = a piece of fruit; **las frutas** = fruit in general.*

When you're asking for something, or offering something, you use **un** or **una**. When you mean *some* you don't need to put anything before the noun in Spanish:

¿Quieres un plátano?
Do you want a banana?

¿Quieres una manzana?
Do you want an apple?

Quiero sandía.
I want some watermelon.

Quiero queso.
I want some cheese.

¿Quieres guisantes?
Do you want some peas?

¡No olvides el helado!

To tell someone <u>not</u> to do something you use **no** before the verb. If you're using **vosotros** the verb will usually end with **-éis** (if the infinitive ends in **-ar**) or **-áis** (if it ends in **-er** or **-ir**). Similarly if you're using **tú** the verb will usually end with **-es** or **-as**.

¡No toques! / ¡No toquéis!
Don't touch!

¡No te olvides de hacer los deberes!
Don't forget to do your homework!

Language Practice

Whole class activity: preferences

Ask children which fruit or vegetable they prefer:

Andrés, ¿qué te gustan más, las fresas o las manzanas?

Ana, ¿qué te gustan más, las zanahorias o los tomates?

(If anyone hates both they can say **No me gustan ni las zanahorias ni los tomates.**)

Pair activity

It's important to get your healthy 5-a-day-fruit and vegetables, even when you're in Spain! Get the pairs to make a shopping list in Spanish of 5 fruits and vegetables they both like, then choose one person to read it out to the class.

Whole class activity: the top five

Give each child a picture of a different fruit or vegetable and a name to go with it: **Mario, tu eres el señor Zanahoria**; **Maria, tu eres la señora Manzana** etc.

Then get the pairs to read out the lists they made earlier, eg **los plátanos**, **las patatas**, **los tomates**, **las manzanas**, **las fresas**. All the children whose fruit or vegetable appears on the list get a point, so **el señor Plátano, la señora Patata** etc mark 1 on their scoresheets.

When all the pairs have read out their lists, see which fruits and vegetables are the most popular: **Señor Plátano, ¿cuántos puntos tienes?** etc. Write the most popular items on the board under the headings **1º**, **2º**, **3º**, **4º**, **5º**.

EN EL RESTAURANTE

Grammar Background

Tener...

In Spanish you use the verb **tener** to say that you're hungry or thirsty, and hot or cold:

¿Tienes sed? Are you thirsty?	**Tengo mucha sed.** I'm very thirsty.
¿Tienes hambre? Are you hungry?	**No, no tengo hambre.** No, I'm not hungry.

¡Cierra la ventana, tengo frío!
Shut the window. I'm cold!

¡Abre la ventana, por favor, tengo calor!
Open the window, please. I'm hot!

Asking questions

When you ask a question in English you usually put the verb first, eg *Can I help you?* In a statement the verb does not come first (eg *I can help you*).

You can put the verb first in Spanish questions too: **¿es para tí esta sopa?**.

Alternatively you can just make a statement in a questioning tone of voice: **¿Esta sopa es para tí?**. This is common in spoken language, and is how the waiter asks questions in this scene:

¿Esta sopa es para tí?
Is the soup for you?

In Spanish you sometimes start a question by mentioning the thing you're going to ask about:

La sopa, ¿para quién es?
Who's the soup for?

Su chaqueta, ¿de qué color es?
What colour is her jacket?

You may find that this type of question works well in the classroom, since it gives a clear signal what the question is going to be about:

Un aguacate, ¿qué es?
What is 'un aguacate'?

Esa chica, ¿quién es?
Who's that girl?

Un zumo de naranja, ¿cuánto es?
How much is an orange juice?

Language Awareness

Some of the children might notice that there are two things in the picture on p. 38 that are called **unas patatas fritas** and that it might be a mistake. In fact **patatas fritas** can mean two things in Spanish: *crisps* (in the bowl) and *chips* (on the plate with the hamburger).

When the waiter gives Miguel the soup he says **Que aproveche**. This is the Spanish way of saying *Enjoy your meal* or *Bon appétit*.

Language Practice

Game: ¿Quién es? (*Who is it?*)

Can the class guess who you're thinking about? (Be careful not to look at the person!).

They can ask questions about the person's clothes, where they're sitting, their hobbies etc.

¿Tiene un jersey azul?, ¿Toca el piano?, ¿Está enfrente de Pedro?, Está detrás de Irene?, ¿Juega al fútbol?, ¿No le gusta la fruta?, ¿Siempre llega tarde?, ¿Tiene una mochila verde?, ¿Se llama Elena? etc

If they use adjectives, they need to use the feminine or masculine forms once they know if the person is a girl or a boy:

¿Es alta?, **¿Es baja?**, **¿Es delgado?** etc

You could also ask a child to think of a person, and to answer the questions from the class. Get them to whisper the name to you first so you can help if necessary.

EL TIEMPO LIBRE

➲ ***See p. 32 for a photocopiable activity relating to this topic.***

Grammar Background

Look at this dialogue on p. 27:

Elena **¿Cuál es tu día preferido?** (*Which is your favourite day?*)

Miguel **El domingo.**

Elena **¿Por qué?**

Miguel **Porque los domingos no voy a la escuela.**

➲ ***See p. 31 for a photocopiable activity on "por qué" and "porque".***

Note that **los domingos** means both *Sundays* and *on Sundays.*

Miguel has a negative reason for liking Sundays: **No voy**... To make negative sentences you put **no** before the verb.

The class may have positive reasons for liking a particular day:

Los domingos voy a la piscina.
On Sundays I go to the swimming pool

Los sábados hago lo que quiero.
On Saturdays I can do what I like.

Los fines de semana juego con mis amigos.
At weekends I play with my friends.

Language Practice

¿Cuál es tu día preferido?

Revise the days of the week – the class could recite them in chorus. Then ask a few children **¿Cuál es tu día preferido?**. If the first three or four all say **el sábado,** ask **¿Todo el mundo prefiere el sábado?** (*Does everyone like Saturday best?*).

If there are other favourites write **el sábado, el domingo** etc on the board, and see how many votes each day gets.

(!) Remember that the days of the week do not have capital letters in Spanish.

Sentence building – remembering how words fit together

1 ¿Por qué prefieres el sábado? → Porque no voy a la escuela.

You can teach this as the answer and practise it. Then write it on the board with one word missing: **Porque no ____ a la escuela.** Get the class to read it out, adding the missing word. Then rub out another word: **Porque no _______ a la _______**. Keep going until there are only lines on the board to show where the words should be, and the class are chanting the whole sentence from memory.

2 ¿Por qué prefieres el sábado? → Porque los sábados hago lo que quiero.

This answer may look too complicated for your class, but they know all the words. The only problem is stringing them together in the right order. In Spanish sentences like this, the day of the week comes at the beginning of the sentence.

Variation

Make a set of cards each bearing one word from the sentence, ie **porque, los, sábados, hago, lo, que, quiero**, and give each child a word. When you point to the words in the sentence, the children with **porque** shout their word, and so on. After a few practices, rub out the sentence and see if they can still do it. If they have mastered it you can swap the cards around and have another go.

Language Awareness

Words that have more than one meaning: alto

Ask the children to look at what the owl is saying on p. 41. What do they think the last word (**alta**) means? They might think that **alta** = *tall* if they remember that Javier was described as **alto** on p. 23. Why do they think the owl might be covering his ears? Could it be because the music is too *loud*? Could **alto** mean both *tall* and *loud*? Ask the children to look up **alto** to check. When everyone has found the word ask how many meanings **alto** has (2: tall, loud).

EN EL CIRCO

Grammar Background

Plurals

With most Spanish nouns, an **-s** is added to form the plural, eg **una niña, dos niñas**. With other nouns, such as those ending in **-r**, **-n** or **-l**, the letters **-es** are added instead, eg **un domador, dos domadores; un león, dos leones; un animal, dos animales**.

Notice that the word **león** loses its accent in the plural. The same applies to other words with the same ending: **un ratón, dos ratones; un melón, dos melones**.

Pronouns

The word **los** means both *the* and *them*:

¿Ves a los payasos? Sí, los veo. (*Can you see the clowns? Yes, I can see them.*)

When **los**/**las** means *them* it goes in front of the verb, eg **Los conozco** (*I know them*), **Las veo** (*I can see them*). The only exception to this is when the verb is an imperative: **¡Míralos!** (*Look at them!*)

The word **la** means both *the* and *her*:

¿Ves a Fátima? Sí la veo.
(Can you see Fatima? Yes, I can see her.)

For *him*, use the word **lo**:

¿Ves a Marcos? Sí, lo veo.
(Can you see Mark? Yes, I can see him.)

Language Practice

Whole class practice

The class need to know the phrases **lo conozco**; **la conozco**; **los conozco**; **las conozco** (*I know him*; *I know her*; *I know them*) for these exercises.

Teacher **Sonia, ¿conoces a Javier?** →
Sonia **Sí, lo conozco.**

Teacher **Javier, ¿conoces a Sonia?** →
Javier **Sí, la conozco.**

Teacher **Andrés, ¿conoces a Javier y Sonia?** →
Andrés **Sí, los conozco.**

Teacher **Raúl, ¿conoces a Marta y Sonia?** →
Raúl **Sí, las conozco**

When the class has mastered the pronouns, change the pattern, so that the person who answers chooses who to ask next:

Teacher **Ester, ¿conoces a María?**

Ester **Sí, la conozco. Ana, ¿conoces a Álvaro?**

Ana **Sí, lo conozco. Pablo, ¿conoces a Cristina y Daniel?**

Pablo **Sí, los conozco. Paula, ¿conoces a Cristina y Natalia?**

Paula **Sí, las conozco.**

(!) *Note that you use the masculine form **los** when referring to male and female at the same time.*

More difficult variation

¿Ves…? The answer to this may be *yes* or *no* (tell the children not to look around).

If the answer is *no*, children need to add **no** to the sentence, putting **no** in front of **lo, la, los** or **las**: **no lo veo**; **no la veo**; **no los veo**; **no las veo**:

Teacher **Alicia, ¿ves a Carlos?** →
Alicia **Sí, lo veo.**

Teacher **Sara, ¿ves a Alicia?** →
Sara **No, no la veo.**

LA TORMENTA

Language Awareness

The word **la tormenta** looks like the English word *torment* – do the class know what it means? If they know that torment means *extreme suffering* they should realise that **tormenta** is one of those words in Spanish that, although it looks like an English word, means something different; in this case it's *storm*. Other words may be more obvious: **el sol** is like the start of the English word *solar* – a solar eclipse is an eclipse of the sun, a solar panel collects heat from the sun. **La luna** starts like the word *lunar* – a lunar landing is a landing on the moon.

Syllables

Are the Spanish words longer or shorter than the English words? Is there any difference in length between **el sol** and *the sun*? What about **primavera** and *spring*? The Spanish word has four syllables so it takes a lot longer to say than *spring*, which has only one. **Paraguas** and *umbrella* are similar because they have the same number of syllables (3) and the stress also goes on the same syllable in both languages.

If the class is not familiar with the term 'syllable', demonstrate how words can be divided up: com-pu-ter; un-ne-ces-sa-ry; sci-en-ti-fi-cal-ly.

Get them to write their names divided up into syllables, working in pairs so they can help each other. Have some of them read out their names: Pe-ne-lo-pe Ro-bin-son etc. See who has the most syllables in their first name. How many people's names have only one syllable? (eg Paul, Anne, Mark, Luke, Claire, Jack).

Then give them half a dozen words they've learned recently to divide up – for example, **plátano**, **pepino**, **tomate**, **fresa**, **melón**, **manzana** (plá-ta-no, pe-pi-no, to-ma-te, fre-sa, me-lón, man-za-na).

➲ ***See p. 31 for a photocopiable exercise on counting syllables.***

Grammar Background

Las estaciones

la primavera the spring →
en primavera in the spring

el verano the summer →
en verano in the summer

el otoño the autumn →
en otoño in the autumn

el invierno the winter →
en invierno in the winter

¿Qué estación....? Which season...?

ⓘ *Note that the names of months and seasons do not have capital letters in Spanish.*

Language Practice

Whole class practice

Revise the months of the year by asking what season they are:

¿Es invierno en enero? Sí.

¿Es invierno en abril? No, es primavera.

Pair work

Get the children to ask each other about the seasons and months of their birthdays:

¿Tu cumpleaños es en invierno?
(*Is your birthday in the winter?*) → **No.**

¿Tu cumpleaños es en primavera?
(*Is your birthday in the spring?*) → **Sí.**

¿En abril? → **No.**

¿En mayo? → **Sí.**

Then ask them to report back to the class:

Teacher: **Jorge, ¿el cumpleaños de Luis cuándo es?**

Jorge: **Es en primavera, en mayo.**

LA NATURALEZA

Grammar Background

The phrase **hay** means *there is/there are*.

Language Practice

¿Tienes buena memoria?

Tell the class they're going to draw a picture – the one on p. 47 of the dictionary. Give them three minutes to look at it and listen to you saying the words. They should repeat the words after you to help them remember the details. When the three minutes are up they can start drawing (it doesn't have to be detailed). Describe the picture to jog their memories:

Hay un árbol; en el árbol hay un nido.

En el nido hay tres pajaritos.

Hay un pájaro grande que les da de comer.

En el árbol también hay un búho.

Debajo del árbol hay una tienda de campaña.

Debajo del nido, a la derecha hay una araña.

Al lado del árbol hay un niño y una niña.

Delante del niño y la niña hay una rana.

A la derecha hay un hombre y una mujer.

Alternatively, if you think the class would find so much Spanish overwhelming, you could do it like this:

No olvidéis el árbol.
(Don't forget the tree.)

No olvidéis el búho.
(Don't forget the owl.)

When they've finished their drawings, let them look at the picture, and go over the words again, checking who remembered each detail:

¿Quién tiene el árbol?
(Who's got the tree?)

¿Quién tiene la tienda de campaña?
(Who's got the tent?)

Bravo to anyone who remembered **la pluma**, **las hojas**, or **la carretera**!

La geografía

Ask children which geographical words in "**La geografía**" insert they recognise. Then put these categories on the board and see if the class can give you an example of each:

un continente – **un desierto** – **una isla** – **un mar** – **un océano** – **una selva** – **un volcán**

Then ask the whole class questions to help you correctly fill in each category:

¿Qué es el Pacífico: un mar o un océano?

¿Qué es el Etna: un volcán o una isla?

¿Qué es el Sáhara: una selva o un desierto?

Some suggestions:

deserts:	**Gobi, Kalahari;**
islands:	**Tenerife, Creta;**
seas:	**Caribe, Mediterráneo;**
oceans:	**Atlántico, Índico;**
jungles:	**Amazonas;**
volcanoes:	**Vesubio, Krakatoa.**

If the class don't recognize a word, help them spot similarities to the English.

LAS VACACIONES

Grammar Background

¿Dónde vas? (*Where are you going?*)

✱ **Voy a...**

When you're talking about going <u>to a place</u> the word for *to* is generally **a**:

Voy a la montaña.
I'm going to the mountains.

Voy a la playa/a Madrid.
I'm going to the seaside/to Madrid.

Tengo que ir al médico.
I have to go to the doctor's.

(!) *Note that in Spanish you wouldn't say <u>Voy a las montañas</u> in this case, although we use the plural in English.*

The definite article **el**/**la** (the) is used in the same way in Spanish and English, **a** + **el** becoming **al** when it's before a masculine noun. An exception to this is **correos**, when the article is not used:

Voy <u>a</u> correos.
I'm going to the post office.

✱ **Voy a casa de...**

When the place you're going to is someone's <u>house</u>, the word for *to* is **a casa de**:

Voy a casa de Miguel
I'm going to Miguel's (house).

Voy a casa de mis abuelos.
I'm going to my grandparents' (house).

¿Qué vas a hacer? (*What are you going to do?*)

Voy a jugar en la playa.
I'm going to play on the beach.

Voy a nadar en el mar.
I'm going to swim in the sea.

Using the Dictionary

In this dictionary all forms of the verbs, or "doing words", have an entry, eg **coge**, **eres**, **siéntate**. However, at this type of entry you'll see an arrow symbol referring you to the *main entry* for the verb, which is in the infinitive form (**coger**, **ser**, **sentarse**), where you will find the translation and any examples. Look at the sentence **Voy a la montaña** on p. <u>49</u>. If the children look the word **Voy** up they'll see that they have to go to the entry for **ir** (*to go*) to find information on this verb.

Language Practice

Las vacaciones de tus sueños (*Your dream holiday*)

Ask for (or teach) some names of continents, countries and activities, write them on the board and have a vote to find which are the most popular.

Continente	País	Actividad
Australia	España	el camping
Europa	Portugal	la bici
América	Francia	la playa
África	Italia	el esquí
Asia	Grecia	la piscina

Yo prefiero la playa...

With the list of activities on the board, you can now ask about individual preferences:

Andrés, ¿que prefieres, la playa o la piscina?
(Which do you prefer...)

Prefiero la montaña.
(I prefer...)

Rosa, ¿qué prefieres, el camping o la bici?
Prefiero el camping.

Now pairs can work together to choose.

LA FIESTA

Grammar Background

The word **su** means both *his* and *her.*

Luis y su padre
Luis and his father

Emma y su madre
Emma and her mother

It can also mean *their*:

Elena, Miguel y su madre
Elena, Miguel and their mother

You use the plural adjective **sus** with plural nouns:

Elena y sus amigas
Elena and her friends

Miguel y sus amigos
Miguel and his friends

Elena, Miguel y sus padres
Elena, Miguel and their parents

To say *Javier's friends* in Spanish, you literally say *the friends of Javier:* **los amigos de Javier**.

el cumpleaños de Miguel
Miguel's birthday
→ **su cumpleaños**
his birthday

la fiesta de Miguel
Miguel's party
→ **su fiesta**
his party

los regalos de Miguel
Miguel's presents
→ **sus regalos**
his presents

Language Practice

Whole class practice: Es mi cumpleaños (It's my birthday)

Find out if it's anyone's birthday today , or if anyone has one coming up.

Teacher **¿Hoy es el cumpleaños de alguien?**

Child **Sí, es mi cumpleaños.**

Teacher **¿Mañana es el cumpleaños de alguien?**

Child **Sí, es mi cumpleaños mañana.**

Teacher **¿El sábado es el cumpleaños de alguien?**

Alternatively, if you have a birthday list of your class you can ask about dates that will interest them:

El uno de junio, ¿de quién es el cumpleaños?

El doce de enero, ¿de quién es el cumpleaños?

To make it easier, point to dates on the calendar when asking the questions.

Pair practice: other people's birthdays

Pairs ask each other **¿Cuándo es tu cumpleaños?** and make a note of the answer, writing down the date in the Spanish way, eg **el cinco de abril**.

You then prompt each person to tell the class about their partner:

El cumpleaños de Marcos es el cinco de abril.

Homework

Write a Spanish invitation to a party for your next birthday. You may need to change **cinco** to another word such as **tres** or **cuatro**. Look on p. 94 for more words like this. Remember to change the month too!

Who are you going to invite? Here are some possibilities: **mi madre, mi padre, mi primo, mi prima, mi abuela, mi abuelo, mi hermano, mi hermana, mi tía, mi tío, mi amigo, mi amiga**. Make **una lista de invitados** (a guest list).

ALPHABETICAL ORDER 1

a b c d e f g h i j k l m n o p q r s t u v w x y z

EXERCISE 1

Raúl is a young wizard who's learning spells at school. He knows the spell that turns dragons into kittens is something like **enero septiembre octubre noviembre.** But the dragon is getting closer and closer, and the spell isn't working! "Try alphabetical order!" suggests his friend Raquel.

1 ______________ 2 ______________ 3 ______________ 4 ______________

Phew! Just in time.

There's another spell for snakes, something like **marzo enero abril noviembre**. Can you put these words in the right order for Raúl?

1 ______________ 2 ______________ 3 ______________ 4 ______________

[When there are words starting with the same letter in a list, such as John, Jane and Jill, you have to look at the <u>second</u> letter to put them in order: J<u>a</u>ne, J<u>i</u>ll, J<u>o</u>hn.]

Raúl is sure he's got the rolling rock spell right: **agosto abril mayo septiembre** – but he hasn't! Can you make it right?

1 ______________ 2 ______________ 3 ______________ 4 ______________

[When there are words starting with the same two letters in a list, such as Jane, Jack and Jaqueline, you have to look at the <u>third</u> letter to put them in order: Ja<u>c</u>k, Ja<u>n</u>e, Ja<u>q</u>ueline.]

This time the whole school is shaking because a giant is hammering on the door. Raúl knows the words in the spell to fix giants are **abril junio mayo marzo**, so why is the giant still there? Quick, help him correct the alphabetical order!

1 ______________ 2 ______________ 3 ______________ 4 ______________

EXERCISE 2

> Riddle: When does Friday come before Thursday?
>
> When it's in alphabetical order!

This is the order we usually put the days of the week in: Monday, Tuesday, Wednesday, Thursday, Friday, Saturday, Sunday. Can you put them in <u>alphabetical</u> order?

1 ______________ 2 ______________ 3 ______________ 4 ______________

5 ______________ 6 ______________ 7 ______________

Now see if you can complete this riddle:

> When is ______________________ the last day of the week?
>
> When it's in alphabetical order!

ALPHABETICAL ORDER 2

a b c d e f g h i j k l m n o p q r s t u v w x y z

EXERCISE 1

Celia is never ready on time. She can never find anything because her room is such a mess. Maybe if her wardrobe was in alphabetical order it would help. Can you sort her clothes out? There's a **skirt**, an **anorak**, **trousers**, a **dress**, a **coat** and a **jacket**.

1 ___________ 2 ___________ 3 ___________ 4 ___________ 5 ___________ 6 ___________

Now can you write the Spanish words for these clothes?

1 ___________ 2 ___________ 3 ___________ 4 ___________ 5 ___________ 6 ___________

That's spoilt her nice tidy alphabetical order – can you sort it out for her again?

1 ___________ 2 ___________ 3 ___________ 4 ___________ 5 ___________ 6 ___________

EXERCISE 2

What colour are the clothes?

You can find out by putting these colours into alphabetical order.

rosa, verde, azul, rojo

1 ___________ 2 ___________ 3 ___________ 4 ___________

Now put colour number one in sentence 1, and so on.

1 El jersey es ___________. 2 Es vestido es ___________.

3 El abrigo es ___________. 4 La camiseta es ___________.

Can you find what these colours are called in English?

1 ___________ 2 ___________ 3 ___________ 4 ___________

Are they still in alphabetical order? Can you sort them out?

1 ___________ 2 ___________ 3 ___________ 4 ___________

EXERCISE 3

Can you complete the words to make the alphabet? There is only one word beginning with **k** in the dictionary – can you find it and put it in the gap?

a _ _ _ _ *(friend)* **b** _ _ _ _ *(good)* **c** _ _ _ *(bed)* **d** _ _ *(day)* **e** _ _ _ _ *(january)*

f _ _ _ _ *(skirt)* **g** _ _ _ *(cat)* **h** _ _ _ *(time)* **i** _ *(go)* **j** _ _ _ _ _ *(Thursday)*

k _ _ _ _ _ _(...) **l** _ _ _ _ *(pencil)* **m** _ _ _ *(mother)* **n** _ _ _ _ *(black)*

o _ _ *(bear)* **p** _ _ _ _ *(father)* **q** _ _ *(what)* **r** _ _ _ _ *(mouse)*

s _ _ _ _ *(seven)* **t** _ _ _ _ _ _ *(toast)* **u** _ _ *(one)* **v** _ _ _ *(cow)*

w **x** **y** _ *(I)* **z** _ _ _ *(juice)*

USING THE DICTIONARY

EXERCISE 1

Sí, por favor or No gracias?

Miguel and his cat Félix don't always like the same things to eat and drink. For each item in the list below, write **sí** if you think Miguel or Félix would like it, and **no** if they wouldn't. Look up any words you don't know in the dictionary.

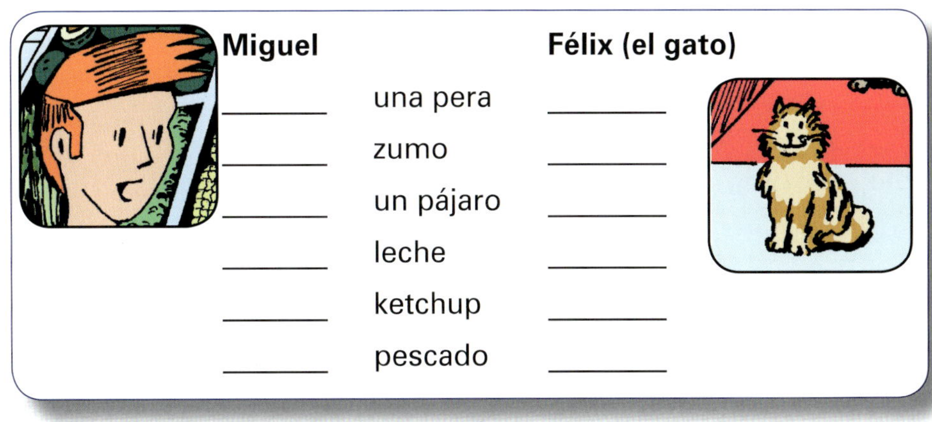

Miguel		Félix (el gato)
______	una pera	______
______	zumo	______
______	un pájaro	______
______	leche	______
______	ketchup	______
______	pescado	______

Now answer these questions with **Sí, por favor** or **No gracias**:

¿Quieres zumo, Tomás? ____________

¿Quieres una pera, Félix? ____________

EXERCISE 2

Javier is a vegetarian. Tick the things he will eat.

cerdo	un plátano	espaguetis	patatas
tomates	cerezas	jamón	cereales
fresas	salchichas	avocados	miel

Elena is on a strange diet – she only eats red things!

What are the three things she will eat from the list above?

________ __________ ____________

EXERCISE 3

¡Peligro! ¡Tiburones! Should you run away, call the police, hide, or what?

Do you know the meaning of **tiburones**? If not, quick! – look it up in the dictionary before it's too late, and tick the right warning.

☐ Don't light a fire here.

☐ Don't swim here.

☐ Don't touch anything here.

EXERCISE 4

Congratulations! You've won a Spanish raffle.
You can choose one of these prizes:

una cometa

unos patines

una bicicleta

Use the dictionary if you're not sure what the prizes are. Then write your choice in the gap.

Quiero __ __________________ por favor.

¡LLEGAMOS TARDE!

Rosa, Tomás, Marcos, María, Diego and Lucas are all late for work.

Do you know what their jobs are? Use your dictionary if you don't know all the words.

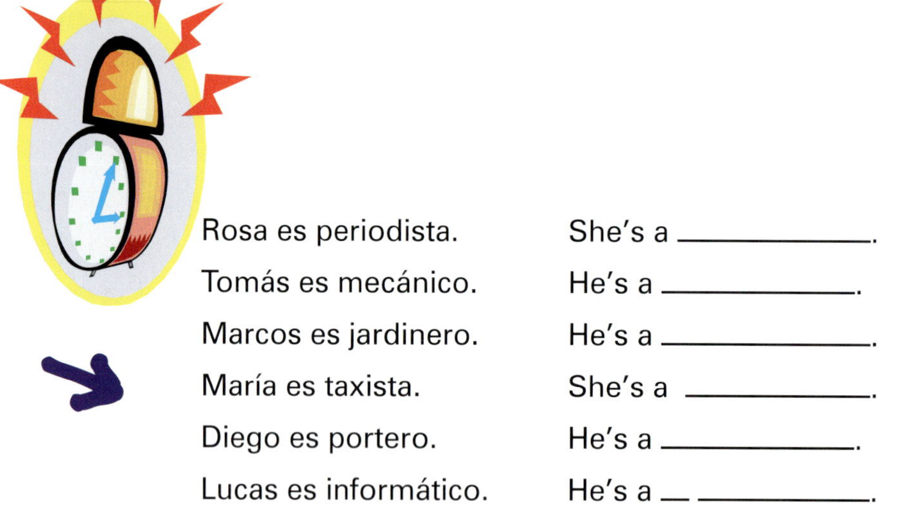

Rosa es periodista. She's a ____________.

Tomás es mecánico. He's a ____________.

Marcos es jardinero. He's a ____________.

María es taxista. She's a ____________.

Diego es portero. He's a ____________.

Lucas es informático. He's a __ ____________.

They're all late because they can't find one vital thing they need to do their job.

Can you work out who would use each of the things below, and write their name in the gap?

Toma tu destornillador, ...

Toma tus llaves, ...

Toma tu balón, ...

Toma tus tijeras, ...

Toma tu ratón, ...

Toma tu micrófono, ...

WORDS THAT RHYME

EXERCISE 1

Does your name rhyme with any other word?

The name *Mark* rhymes with lots of words – can you think of some?

....

What about *Penelope* – does that rhyme with anything?

Ramón and **Teresa** are Spanish names that rhyme with other words:

A Ra<u>món</u> le gusta el ja<u>món</u>.

Ter<u>esa</u> quiere una hamburgu<u>esa</u>.

EXERCISE 2

¿Quién es? (*Who is it?*)

Can you find the name that rhymes with the bold word in the question? Write it in the gap.

¿Quién está mirando la **ballena**? __________ Eulalia / Magdalena

¿Quién está en el **hospital**? __________ Ramiro / Marcial / Osvaldo

¿Quién está en el **mar**? __________ Victoria / Ana / Pilar

¿Quién está en el **aeropuerto**? __________ Arturo / Enrique / Alberto

¿Quién está en la **piscina**? __________ Elena / Marina / Julia

EXERCISE 3

Odd one out

Three of the bold words (or bits of words) in the boxes rhyme, and one doesn't. Cross out the one that doesn't.

Pon el **plato** en la mesa.
Veo un **pato** en el jardín.
Bebo un **vaso** de agua.
El **gato** salta sobre la caja.

Pablo tiene **tres** hermanos.
Tengo **diez** años.
Hay un **pez** en el agua.
Tiene una ca**bez**a grande.

Ha perdido un **diente**.
Hay **veinte** niños.
La sopa está ca**liente**.
¿Ves el **puente**?

¿Dónde está tu a**brigo**?
Mi a**migo** viene hoy.
Su **hijo** está en la escuela.
Ro**drigo** vive cerca de aquí.

THE SAME BUT DIFFERENT...

EXERCISE 1

Hospital, piano, animal, doctor, hotel, actor, radio...

... lots of words look the same in Spanish and English, and mean the same thing. But some words can trick you: they look the same, but they mean something different: for example, **un pie** means *a foot* in Spanish, not *a pie*.

Here are some tricky words – can you find the right words in the box to complete the sentences?

clothes, container for flowers, suffering, shape, nice, storm, number, compassionate, address book, list of matters for discussion at a meeting, glass, thick cord

Spanish	English
Una agenda is an ________.	An agenda is a ________.
Una figura is a ________.	A figure is a ________.
Un vaso is a ________.	A vase is a ________.
Ropa is ________.	Rope is ________.
Una tormenta is a ________.	Torment is ________.
Simpático means ________.	Sympathetic means ________.

EXERCISE 2

Some lookalike words mean the same thing, but are spelled differently: for example, **diccionario** has two **c**'s, and a different ending from *dictionary.*

Write the English for these Spanish words, without looking in the dictionary.

Spanish	English	Spanish	English
un supermercado	________	una jirafa	________
el tenis	________	un tomate	________
noviembre	________	un trompeta	________
una guitarra	________	el tigre	________
una patata	________	un yogur	________

Now check your English spelling by looking up the Spanish words in the dictionary.

What was your score out of 10?

____

10/10 ¡Excelente!
9/10 ¡Muy bien!
8/10 ¡Bien!
7/10 ¡Bastante bien!
Menos de 6/10 Hmm

¿POR QUÉ HACES ESO?

Why are you doing that?

Here are some silly answers about why people are doing things.
Can you match up the real answer to each question?

1 ¿Por qué te comes un sándwich?	A Porque es sábado
2 ¿Por qué te ríes?	B Porque hace frío.
3 ¿Por qué bebes zumo de naranja?	C Porque llego tarde.
4 ¿Por qué lloras?	D Porque es divertido.
5 ¿Por qué llevas abrigo?	E Porque quiero nadar.
6 ¿Por qué abres la ventana?	F Porque no quiero.
7 ¿Por qué vas a la piscina?	G Porque tengo mucha hambre.
8 ¿Por qué corres?	H Porque estoy triste.
9 ¿Por qué no vienes?	I Porque tengo sed.
10 ¿Por qué no vas a la escuela?	J Porque hace mucho calor.

SYL-LA-BLE SA-FA-RI PARK

Syl-la-ble Sa-fa-ri Park is an interesting place – all the animals are Spanish, and it has three enclosures: Area One is for animals with two-syllable names, Area Two is for animals with three-syllable names and Area Three is for all the others. Can you put these new arrivals in the right Area?

Area One	Area Two	Area Three

una jirafa
un hipopótamo
un elefante
un oso
un león
una foca
un cocodrilo
un pingüino
un tigre
un tiburón
un gorila
un pez
una mariposa

EN MI OPINIÓN...

In my opinion...

Here are 12 ways of spending your time. Are they good things to do? Tick the opinion you agree with most.

Use the dictionary if you don't understand a word.

! Tip: Es mejor que ... means *It's better than...*

jugar al golf es...
- ☐ divertido
- ☐ imposible
- ☐ muy difícil
- ☐ no muy divertido

aprender español es...
- ☐ divertido
- ☐ difícil pero divertido
- ☐ divertido y fácil
- ☐ imposible

comer un helado es...
- ☐ difícil
- ☐ muy fácil
- ☐ divertido
- ☐ peligroso

ir a la escuela es...
- ☐ interesante
- ☐ no muy divertido
- ☐ mejor que nadar con tiburones
- ☐ interesante y divertido

nadar es...
- ☐ divertido
- ☐ genial
- ☐ difícil
- ☐ no muy divertido

un videojuego es...
- ☐ interesante
- ☐ mejor que jugar al fútbol
- ☐ mejor que las matemáticas
- ☐ difícil

bailar es...
- ☐ fácil
- ☐ muy fácil
- ☐ peligroso
- ☐ no muy divertido

construir casas es...
- ☐ muy divertido
- ☐ imposible
- ☐ fácil
- ☐ difícil

ir de vacaciones es...
- ☐ divertido
- ☐ no muy divertido
- ☐ interesante
- ☐ mejor que ir a la escuela

ir en canoa es...
- ☐ muy fácil
- ☐ difícil
- ☐ imposible
- ☐ genial

tocar la guitarra es...
- ☐ imposible
- ☐ muy difícil
- ☐ genial
- ☐ divertido

cantar es...
- ☐ difícil
- ☐ mejor que bailar
- ☐ no muy divertido
- ☐ muy divertido

Which of the 12 activities do you like best? Put your favourite in the box, and two adjectives in the gaps.

En mi opinión, ________________ es ____________________ y ________________